Careers without College

Photographer

by *Kathryn A. Quinlan*

Consultant:

Jeff Lubin
Portrait Photographer
Contributing Artist to *Storytellers*,
Magazine of the Professional Photographers of America

CAPSTONE
HIGH/LOW BOOKS
an imprint of Capstone Press
Mankato, Minnesota

Capstone High/Low Books are published by Capstone Press
818 North Willow Street, Mankato, Minnesota 56001
http://www.capstone-press.com

Library of Congress Cataloging-in-Publication Data
Quinlan, Kathryn A.
    Photographer/by Kathryn A. Quinlan.
    p. cm. — (Careers without college)
    Includes bibliographical references (p. 44) and index.
    Summary: Outlines the educational requirements, duties, salary, employment
outlook, and possible future positions for photographers.
    ISBN 0-7368-0176-6
    1. Photography—Vocational guidance—Juvenile literature. [1. Photography—
Vocational guidance. 2. Vocational guidance.] I. Title. II. Series: Careers without
college (Mankato, Minn.)
TR154.Q56 1999
770'.23—dc21   98-45192
                                                                     CIP
                                                                      AC

Editorial Credits
Leah Pockrandt, editor; Steve Christensen, cover designer; Kimberly Danger and
    Sheri Gosewisch, photo researchers

Photo Credits
Dembinsky Photo Association, 31; Skip Moody, 24; Stan Osolinski, 38
Gerald D. Tang, 34
International Stock/Richard Hackett, 29
Jay Ireland & Georgienne E. Bradley, 4, 32, 36
Mike Booher, 20
Photophile/Roger Holden, 19
Photo Network/T.J. Florian, 11; Tom McCarthy, 15
Rainbow/William Stanton, 26
Robin Moyer, 12
Shayds of Color, 16
Transparencies Inc./Jane Faircloth, 9
Unicorn Stock Photos/Chromosohm, 40
Uniphoto/Llewellyn, cover
Visuals Unlimited/Arthur Morris, 6; Barry Slaven, 22

Table of Contents

Fast Facts

Career Title —————————— Photographer

Minimum Educational ———— U.S.: high school diploma
Requirement   Canada: high school diploma

Certification Requirement ——— U.S.: none
                             Canada: none

Salary Range ——————————— U.S.: $14,500 to $75,100
(U.S. Bureau of Labor Statistics and   Canada: $12,100 to $53,600
Human Resources Development   (Canadian dollars)
Canada, late 1990s figures)

Job Outlook ———————————— U.S.: average growth
(U.S. Bureau of Labor Statistics and   Canada: fair
Human Resources Development
Canada, late 1990s projections)

DOT Cluster —————————— Professional, technical, and
(Dictionary of Occupational Titles)   managerial occupations

DOT Numbers —————————— 143.062-030, 143.062-034

GOE Number ——————————— 01.02.03
(Guide for Occupational Exploration)

NOC ——————————————— 5221
(National Occupational Classification—Canada)

Chapter 1

Job Responsibilities

Photographers take photographs of people, places, things, and events. There are many kinds of photographers. Some photographers work for people who want photos taken of themselves or others. Other photographers work for newspapers, advertising companies, and police departments. Photographers can work wherever people want a visual record of people, things, or events.

Photographers must be artistic, creative, and knowledgeable. Good photographers understand how colors and light appear in photos. They know how to arrange objects and people to create interesting photos. Photographers also must know how to use various camera equipment.

Photographers often take photographs of a variety of people in many settings.

On the Job

All photographers must have technical skills. They must understand photography processes. These include how to use camera equipment, develop film, and print photographs.

Photographers need artistic skills. They may take photographs of families, models, products, and scenery. Photographers need to know how to arrange people and objects in photos.

Photographers who work with people also need personal skills. They need to talk to the people they photograph. They also need to talk to the people who want their services. Photographers need to know what types of photos people want.

Photographers can specialize in many areas. These include portrait, scientific, journalistic, and fine art photography.

Portrait Photographers

Portrait photographers take photographs of people. Usually they try to show people looking their best. Portrait photographers often photograph people who

Portrait photographers take photos of people in studios.

are not professional models. These photographers try to help people relax and look natural.

Some portrait photographers take pictures of famous people. These people often have been photographed many times. Portrait photographers try to find new and interesting ways to photograph these

9

people. For example, they may take photographs that show a famous person's hobbies or interests.

Commercial and Industrial Photographers

Businesses sometimes hire commercial photographers to take photos. Businesses usually use these photos to advertise products or services. Commercial photos may be printed in catalogs, magazines, or on billboards. The photos also may be used in TV shows, films, and TV commercials.

Commercial photographers take photos of a variety of things. Some commercial photographers take photos of products such as toys, food, or machines. Others take photographs of models wearing special clothes or makeup.

Businesses use commercial photographs to attract customers. Their photos need to get people's attention. The photos must be clear and carefully arranged.

Industrial photographers take photographs of companies' employees, products, or services. They also may take photos of machinery, buildings, or stores. Companies use these photographs to advertise companies or their products and services.

Photojournalists take photographs to convey information to newspaper and magazine readers.

Commercial and industrial photographers may work for studios, companies, or on a freelance basis. Companies hire freelance photographers for projects.

Photojournalists

Many photographers work for newspapers or magazines. These photographers are photojournalists.

Photojournalists take photographs of a variety of events.

They take photographs to convey news and information to readers.

Photojournalists take photos of many subjects. They take photos of people, places, and events. Some photojournalists travel a great deal. Photojournalists may photograph famous people. They also may photograph natural disasters. Sometimes their photos help to tell stories. Other times their photos tell the stories themselves.

Photojournalists try to give as much information as possible in each photo. Photos sometimes show emotion. For example, a photograph can show a sports team's joy after winning a championship. A photograph also can show a family's grief after losing its home to fire.

Forensic Photographers

Forensic photographers mainly work with police departments. Their photos may be used in trials to help prove something.

Forensic photographers take photos of many subjects. They photograph crime and accident scenes. They also photograph victims and their wounds.

Forensic photographers try to take very detailed photographs. For example, a photographer might place a ruler next to a victim's wound. The ruler will help show the size of the wound in a photo.

Sometimes forensic photographers take pictures during autopsies. Autopsies are studies performed on dead people to establish the cause of death.

Medical and Scientific Photographers

Medical and scientific photographers take photos for science publications, research reports, and textbooks. These photographs may show each step in a scientific or medical process. For example, medical photographers sometimes take photographs of surgeries or the stages of illnesses. Scientific and medical photographers also may show medical or scientific discoveries or experiments.

Fine Art Photographers

Fine art photographers take photographs that express their emotions and ideas. These photographers may try to show familiar objects in new ways. They may try to show different views of the world. Their photographs may help people think in new ways.

Fine art photographers work with many subjects. Some take photographs of things in nature. Some take photos of people or cities. Other fine art photographers take still-life photos of objects. In still photography, objects and models are motionless when photographs are taken. Photographers may take one or more objects and combine them in unusual ways.

Fine art photographers take photos of many subjects.

Fine art photographers may work with color or black-and-white film. They sometimes combine photography with other art forms. For example, some photographers paint colors on their black-and-white photos. Most fine art photographers have their own studios where they create photographs. These photographs may be published in books or sold in art galleries.

Chapter 2

What the Job Is Like

Different photographers have different job duties. Each kind of photography has its own challenges and rewards.

Portrait Photographers

Portrait photographers work in a variety of situations. Many portrait photographers work in studios. Some of these photographers have studios in their homes. Some portrait photographers work in department stores. They take photos of models, families, businesspeople, and others.

Portrait photographers take photos at special events. These include weddings, parties, and

Portrait photographers take photos of families and models in their studios.

graduations. Photographers also take photos at religious ceremonies such as confirmations and bar and bat mitzvahs.

Portrait photographers sometimes work with challenging people. For example, small children may cry when they are photographed. These photographers must be able to help people feel comfortable.

Portrait photographers work varied hours. They often work during evenings and weekends. They must be available to photograph special occasions.

Photographers who are self-employed have some control over their work hours. These freelance photographers work for themselves instead of for businesses or studios. But often they do a great deal of work. They must take the photos, develop the film, and print the photographs themselves. Many portrait photographers do not have assistants to do these duties for them.

Commercial and Industrial Photographers

Commercial photographers often work many hours a day. They must meet tight deadlines. A deadline is the time when a job or piece of work must be finished.

Portrait photographers work with all types of people.

Commercial photographers may work in studios or on location. Some commercial photographers travel frequently. For example, some travel to factories to take photos of machinery. Others go to restaurants or stores to take photos for advertisements.

Most industrial photographers work for large companies. They may travel to different factories, offices, or stores to take photos for advertisements.

Photojournalists must be available at all times.

They usually work regular business hours. But industrial photographers may have to work during weekends or evenings.

Commercial and industrial photographers face several challenges on location. For example, they may have to work with poor lighting, crowded surroundings, or changes in weather. These conditions may make it difficult to take good photos.

Self-employed commercial and industrial photographers may allow stock photo agencies to use their photos. Photographers give these businesses legal permission to use their photos. The agencies show the photographs to publishers and other customers who need photos. The agencies pay the photographers when their photos are used in publications.

Photojournalists

Photojournalists often have the most unusual hours of all photographers. They must be available to take photos whenever news events occur. Photojournalists usually work many hours a day. They also must work quickly to meet deadlines.

Photojournalists must travel to their assignment locations. Some photojournalists travel to different countries to take photographs. They sometimes work in uncomfortable and even dangerous conditions. For example, they may photograph floods, forest fires, and wars. They also sometimes carry heavy camera equipment. They must be in good physical condition to be able to do their work.

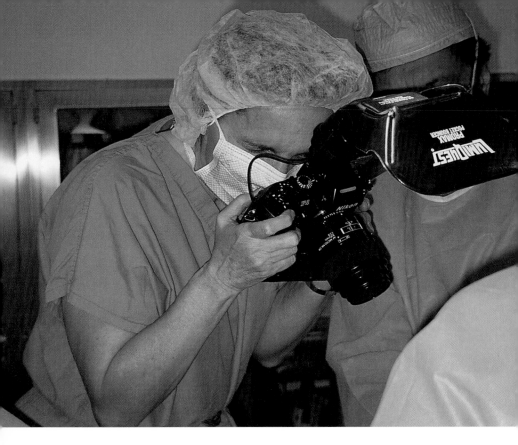

Medical photographers sometimes work in sterile conditions.

Forensic Photographers

Forensic photographers work in a variety of settings. They must photograph crime and accident scenes in all types of weather. They may photograph victims who are upset and in pain.

Forensic photographers work varied hours. For example, those who work for lawyers or insurance companies usually work during the day. But forensic photographers who work for police departments may work days, evenings, and weekends.

Medical and Scientific Photographers

Medical and scientific photographers generally work in clean, bright surroundings. Medical photographers usually work in hospitals, clinics, or universities. Scientific photographers often work in laboratories.

Medical and scientific photographers usually take photos of arranged events. These include surgeries and experiments. Medical and scientific photographers usually work regular business hours.

Medical photographers who photograph surgeries have special challenges. Surgeries must be performed in sterile conditions. All exposed surfaces such as clothing and skin must be free of germs. Medical photographers must make sure their photo equipment is sterile. They also may wear surgical gloves, gowns, and masks. They must not touch or get too close to patients.

Some fine art photographers take nature photos.

Fine Art Photographers

Fine art photographers work in a variety of settings.
Successful fine art photographers may have large
studios with expensive equipment. Beginning fine
art photographers may have small studios and
limited equipment. Fine art photographers who take

nature photos may spend a great deal of time outdoors. Others may photograph different objects in their studios.

Personal Qualities

All photographers need similar skills and personal qualities. All photographers must understand color and design. They must be able to arrange colors and objects in photographs. They also need to know how to use different types of film and light. They need to pay attention to details. They also should have good ideas about how to photograph a variety of situations.

Photographers who photograph people must be able to make them feel comfortable. For example, portrait photographers who work with children must be patient and friendly. They must be sensitive to children's needs.

Freelance photographers need a variety of skills. For example, they must have good business skills. They also must be able to work varied schedules and know how to attract customers.

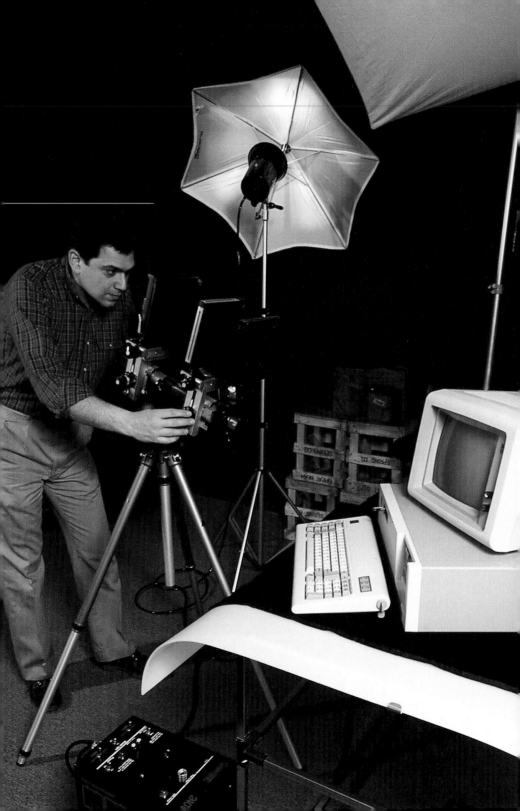

Chapter 3

Training

Careers in photography require training. Different types of photographers need different skills and educational backgrounds.

Most photographers have some formal education. But many photographers simply learn on the job. Many community and junior colleges offer photography courses. Some technical schools, art schools, and universities also offer photography courses. Many employers seek photographers who have some college education.

Some photographers need bachelor's degrees. People earn bachelor's degrees by completing courses of study at colleges or universities. People usually earn bachelor's degrees in four years. Many colleges and universities offer bachelor's degrees in photography.

Photographers may learn on the job.

Many community and junior colleges offer associate's degrees in photography. People earn these degrees by completing programs of study. People usually earn associate's degrees in two years.

Professional photographers need to keep up with new information. They may take classes at schools. Companies that produce photography equipment and supplies may offer classes. Photographers also may read photography publications.

Photographers can gain knowledge through professional groups. Photographers may compete in shows hosted by these groups. Group members also share photography information with one another.

What Photographers Study

Most photography programs offer courses that teach about photography equipment, processes, and styles. Equipment classes teach students how to use different camera lenses, flashes, lights, and filters. A lens is a curved glass in a camera. Lenses bend light and focus images so that they look sharp. Filters are made of glass or plastic. They change the color and light in photos. This gives photographs special moods and

Students learn how to develop and print photographs in process classes.

effects. Different types of photographs require different equipment.

Students study different topics in different classes. Students learn how to develop and print photographs in process classes. Students study style and how to arrange subjects in photographs in technique classes. Different programs teach different elements of photography. For example, art schools might center on design elements of photography. Photojournalism classes might center on news elements of photography.

Photography programs should include some business training. Self-employed photographers must know how to advertise and sell their work. They also must know how to send out bills and order supplies.

Photographers need to know how to protect their legal rights. For example, they need to get permission to take photographs of people. They also must know how to obtain copyright protection for their work. Owners must give permission to others to use copyrighted items. Photographers can learn about copyright information from books or in classes.

What Students Can Do Now

Students interested in photography can gain experience now. Some high schools offer photography classes. Summer camps or after-school programs may offer photography classes. Youth programs such as 4-H and scouting also offer photography opportunities.

Students may get jobs related to photography. They may work at photography stores. Some photographers

Students interested in photography may gain experience through a variety of classes or youth programs.

also hire assistants to help them at weddings. These jobs can help students learn about photography.

The best way to learn photography skills is to take photos. Interested students can volunteer to take photos for their school newspapers or yearbooks. They also can take photos of family events and trips.

Chapter 4

Salary and Job Outlook

Salaries for photographers vary. Photographers in the United States earn between $14,500 and $75,100 (all figures late 1990s). Their average annual salary is between $21,000 and $46,500. Photographers in Canada earn between $12,100 and $53,600. Their average annual salary is about $32,600.

Photographers' salaries depend on the type of work they do. Medical and scientific photographers usually earn higher salaries than other photographers. In general, photographers with more education earn higher salaries.

Self-employed photographers' incomes vary a great deal. Their income often depends upon the economy. Companies tend to spend more money on advertising when the economy is good. Ads often use photos.

Photographers' salaries depend on their specialties.

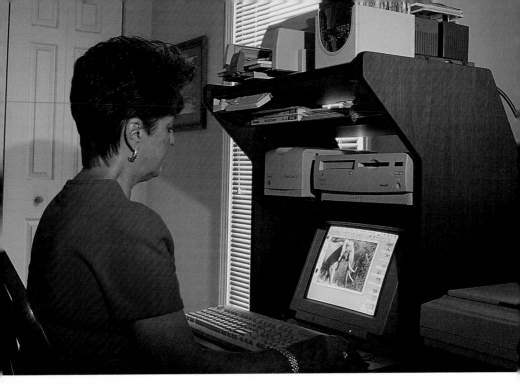

Photographers use computers to alter visual images.

Benefits

Photographers who work for studios or other businesses usually receive salaries and benefits from their employers. Benefits include insurance, retirement plans, and paid sick and vacation time.

Self-employed photographers may not earn a steady income. They also do not receive benefits. These photographers may need to buy their own insurance. They may need to develop their own retirement savings plan.

Outlook

Photography is a competitive career. Many people are interested in photography. Only the most talented photographers succeed.

The photography field is growing at an average rate in the United States. The outlook is fair in Canada.

Recent trends will create work for photographers. For example, schools and businesses are using more visual images. This increased demand will create jobs.

Advances in computer technology mean different opportunities for photographers. More photographers will depend on computer technology. Photographers now can scan images into digital form. They make electronic copies of photographs that can be stored on computers.

Other photographers use digital cameras. These cameras use electronic memory to record images. They do not use film. Digital images are stored on a disk inside the cameras. These images can be viewed using computers. The images can be altered for size or color.

Chapter 5

Where the Job Can Lead

Photographers can advance in many ways. They advance by gaining experience. Some advance as their work becomes well known. Others advance when they take different photography jobs.

Advancement

Portrait photographers may start by working in other people's studios. Some may become part-owners of the studios. Eventually, they may open their own studios.

Commercial and industrial photographers may work for large studios or companies. They advance as they gain experience and responsibility. Some commercial photographers become well known for

Photographers may advance as they gain experience.

Photographers usually receive more interesting assignments as they advance.

their individual styles of work. These photographers may open their own commercial studios.

Photojournalists often start out as photographers for local newspapers. They may advance to larger newspapers or magazines as they gain experience. More experienced photographers usually receive more interesting assignments. For example, sports photographers might begin by photographing high school sports. They then might advance to photographing college or professional sports.

Photojournalists may advance in other ways. For example, some may become photography editors. Other photojournalists may teach at high schools or colleges. These photographers may need teaching degrees.

Forensic photographers advance differently depending on where they work. Photographers who work for insurance companies may get salary increases as they advance. Those who work for police departments may receive higher ranks and earn larger salaries.

Medical and scientific photographers may advance as they gain experience. They may be asked to handle more important jobs. These jobs often pay larger salaries.

Fine art photographers advance as their work becomes well known. They also advance when they sell more photographs and have their photos shown in galleries.

Photography is a competitive profession.

Self-employed photographers advance as they get more customers. They can charge higher prices for their services as they become more well known. Self-employed photographers often hire more people to help them meet their customers' demands.

Other Opportunities

Photography is a challenging profession. Many people try to enter the field each year. Many people who try to become professional photographers do not succeed.

Those who do not become professional photographers may use their skills in other ways. For example, some of these people may become artists at magazines, newspapers, or advertising agencies. Others might work at film processing companies. Still others teach photography or related artistic subjects.

The Future

There will be a need for photographers in the future. This is because of the increased use of visual images in education, communication, and science. The use of computers in photography creates additional job possibilities for photographers.

Photographers need skills, creativity, training, and determination to succeed. Photographers who have artistic skill, an attention to detail, and the desire to do their best can be successful.

Words to Know

autopsy (AW-top-see)—a study performed on a dead person to establish the cause of death

commercial photographer (kuh-MUR-shuhl fuh-TOG-ruh-fur)—a person who takes photographs for businesses

filter (FIL-tur)—an object made of glass or plastic that changes the color and light in photographs

forensic photographer (fuh-REN-sik fuh-TOG-ruh-fur)—a person who takes photos to help prove something

lens (LENZ)—a piece of curved glass in a camera that can bend light and focus images

medical photographer (MED-uh-kuhl fuh-TOG-ruh-fur)—a person who takes photos for science publications, research reports, and textbooks

photojournalist (foh-toh-JURN-uh-list)—a photographer who takes photos of news events

portrait (POR-trit)—a photograph of a person or group of people

studio (STOO-dee-oh)—a room or building in which a photographer works

To Learn More

Cosgrove, Holli, ed. *Career Discovery Encyclopedia*. Vol. 5. Chicago: Ferguson Publishing, 1997.

Evans, Art. *Careers in Photography*. Redondo Beach, Calif.: Photo Data Research, 1992.

Johnson, Bervin M., Robert E. Mayer, and Fred Schmidt. *Opportunities in Photography Careers*.VGM Opportunities Series. Lincolnwood, Ill.: VGM Career Horizons, 1999.

McLean, Cheryl. *Careers for Shutterbugs and Other Candid Types.* VGM Careers for You. Lincolnwood, Ill.: VGM Career Horizons, 1995.

Moss, Miriam. *Fashion Photographer.* Fashion World. New York: Crestwood House, 1991.

Rising, David. *Great Careers for People Interested in Film, Video, and Photography.* Career Connections. Detroit: UXL, 1994.

Useful Addresses

Advertising Photographers of America
7201 Melrose Avenue
Los Angeles, CA 90046

American Society of Media Photographers
14 Washington Road
Suite 502
Princeton Junction, NJ 08550-1033

National Press Photographers Association
3200 Croasdaile Drive
Suite 306
Durham, NC 27705

Professional Photographers of America, Inc.
229 Peachtree Street NE
Suite 2200
Atlanta, GA 30303-2206

Internet Sites

American Society of Media Photographers
http://www.asmp.org

Human Resources Development Canada
http://hrdc-drhc.gc.ca/JobFutures/english/
volume1/522/522.htm

National Press Photographers Association
http://sunsite.unc.edu/nppa

Occupational Outlook Handbook
http://stats.bls.gov/oco/ocos091.htm

Professional Photographers of America, Inc.
http://www.ppa-world.org

Index